W9-AFH-155

GAMES & PUZZLES
You Can Make Yourself

Also by Harvey Weiss:

The Gadget Book
How to Make Your Own Books
Model Airplanes and How to Build Them
Model Cars and Trucks and How to Build Them
Motors and Engines and How They Work
Ship Models and How to Build Them

GAMES & PUZZLES
You Can Make Yourself

HARVEY WEISS

THOMAS Y. CROWELL COMPANY
NEW YORK

Library of Congress Cataloging in Publication Data

Weiss, Harvey.
Games and puzzles you can make yourself.

SUMMARY: Simple text and illustrations introduce
thirty-eight inexpensive, easy-to-make games and puzzles.
1. Games—Juv. lit. 2. Puzzles—Juv.
lit. [1. Games. 2. Puzzles] I. Title.
GV1203.W48   790   75–37886
ISBN 0–690–01111–3

1 2 3 4 5 6 7 8 9 10

Contents

Introduction

The special thing about the games and puzzles in this book is that you can make them yourself. And they are easy to make. In some cases all you need is pencil and paper; or a rubber ball, some string, and a few empty tin cans; or a marble and a few scraps of wood. No special equipment or hard-to-find materials are necessary. In fact, you can make most of the games and puzzles from the odds and ends that are to be found in most households.

One of the big advantages of making your own games and puzzles is that you can change them to suit your own ideas. You don't have to follow the sometimes long, complicated and boring instructions and rules that come with many store-bought games.

To be sure, there are some games and puzzles where fairly exact rules should be followed in order for the action to be most interesting. But in many cases you can make all kinds of changes, or make up the rules for yourself. For example, if you lay out a miniature golf course in your home, you can decide exactly where you want the course to go—through the bedroom or kitchen, up a cardboard ramp, behind the living room sofa, or wherever. In some of the other games it is possible to change the board on which you play—either adding or removing spaces, or altering the paths along which the pieces will move.

There are several games where, if you want to take the time, it is possible to construct good-looking playing boards using permanent materials that are carefully cut out and neatly painted. These make fine gifts. Some of the puzzles, as well as the games, can also be changed to get your own personal variation.

Among the games and puzzles in this book are some that you are no doubt familiar with. Others may be completely unknown to you. But all of them, in one form or another, have been used and enjoyed by peoples of many lands for many years. Some of them in fact are quite ancient. The fox and geese game was first mentioned sometime in the fourteenth century. And variations of this game have been played by the Japanese, the Spaniards, and even the American Indians. Nine-men's morris—an odd name to be sure—was played centuries ago in many different lands. Nobody knows what the game was called in those days. The playing board used in this game has been found carved into the decks of ancient Viking warships.

I. GAMES

Ticktacktoe

Just about everybody has played this game at one time
or another. Most often pencil and paper are used. But it
is more fun to play it with wooden pieces on a wooden
board. If the wood is carefully cut and sanded you can
have a very nice-looking game, ready to take out at a
moment's notice. (See page 8 for some ideas on how to
make a board.)

Two people can play. Each gets five pieces, either circles
or crosses. The players then take turns placing the pieces
on the board. The first one to get three of his pieces in a
row on the board—up and down, across, or on a diagonal
—is the winner. (If you are using pencil and paper, you
take turns making crosses or circles rather than placing
the pieces.)

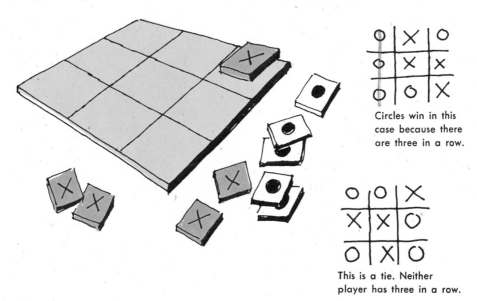

Circles win in this
case because there
are three in a row.

This is a tie. Neither
player has three in a row.

Three-D Ticktacktoe

This is a fancy kind of ticktacktoe that is played on three transparent boards placed one on top of another. The object is to get three of your pieces in a row, just as in regular ticktacktoe, *except* that in this game you can also make a row from *top to bottom*, either in a straight line or on a diagonal. You'll need twelve pieces for each player.

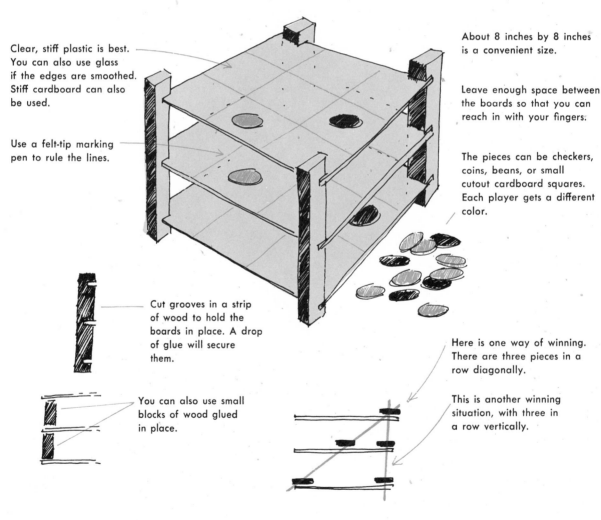

Clear, stiff plastic is best. You can also use glass if the edges are smoothed. Stiff cardboard can also be used.

Use a felt-tip marking pen to rule the lines.

Cut grooves in a strip of wood to hold the boards in place. A drop of glue will secure them.

You can also use small blocks of wood glued in place.

About 8 inches by 8 inches is a convenient size.

Leave enough space between the boards so that you can reach in with your fingers.

The pieces can be checkers, coins, beans, or small cutout cardboard squares. Each player gets a different color.

Here is one way of winning. There are three pieces in a row diagonally.

This is another winning situation, with three in a row vertically.

Dara

This is a game that is very popular in North Africa. It is played by two people on a wooden board that has thirty shallow holes. Each player has twelve pieces, which can be marbles, pebbles, or beans of some sort. The pieces for each player must be in a different color. Instead of a wooden board, you can draw thirty small circles on a piece of paper or cardboard and play on that. Buttons, coins, checkers, or any small flat objects can be used to play with (but you must have twelve of one color and twelve of another).

This is the board for dara. Make sure all the holes, or circles, are in neat, straight rows.

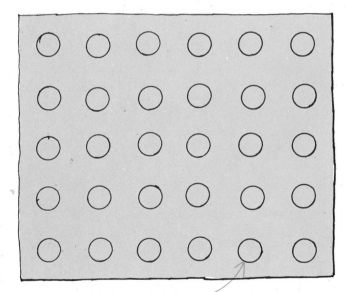

This and some of the other games may at first seem complicated as you read about them. However, once you've made the board and actually started to play against an opponent, you'll immediately see the strategy and tactics that are needed. The more you play, the more challenging the games will become.

With many of these games, where holes are shown in the drawings ruled lines can be used instead.

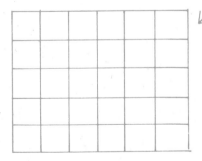

The hole should be big enough to hold securely the marble or whatever playing piece you are using.

The game consists of two parts. In the first part each player takes a turn positioning his men, one at a time, on the board. You are not allowed to place more than two men next to one another during this first part of the game. The first part requires as much thought and planning as the second part, because the placing of the men will decide which future moves are possible.

In the second part of the game the players take turns moving their pieces, one space at a time in any direction *except* diagonally. The purpose is to get three men in a row. When a row of three pieces is formed by one player he removes one of his opponent's pieces. The game is over when one of the players is unable to make any more rows of three, or if all the pieces of one player have been removed.

Here's how a game might look in progress. The player with the orange pieces has a row of three in the lower right-hand corner and can now remove one of his opponent's black pieces.

There is no jumping permitted.

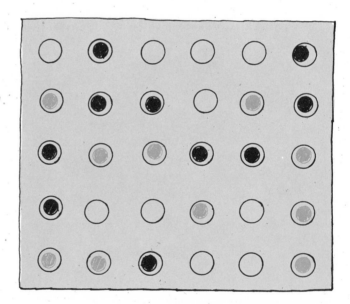

This game is fun to play at the beach, using holes poked in the sand and different-colored pebbles.

6

Go-Bang

Go-bang is a Japanese game quite similar to dara. However, it uses a much larger board and many more pieces. Each player has 100 pieces, and often the game gets quite complex and exciting, with attacks and defenses going on at the same time all over the board. It is great fun.

The pieces are placed anywhere, one at a time, each player taking a turn. The object is to form a straight line of five pieces while at the same time trying to block your opponent's efforts to do the same thing. The five-piece line can be up and down, across, or on a diagonal. If all the pieces are placed on the board and neither player has five in a row, the game may be continued by taking turns moving one piece at a time. No diagonal moves permitted. When a row of five is formed the game is over.

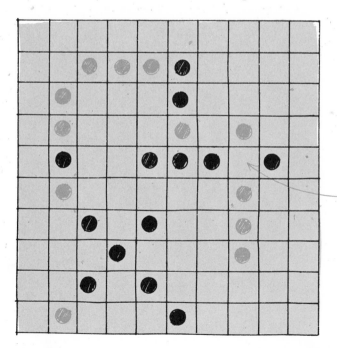

Because there are so many squares on the board you'll have to use small pieces to play with. Small pebbles or beans are suitable.

If it is orange's turn and he places a piece here he will form a row of five and at the same time keep black from getting a row of five.

7

How to Make Playing Boards

Although several of the games described on the previous pages and the next few pages can be played on a board of paper or cardboard having lines ruled with a pencil or marking pen, it is much more fun to use a wooden board, which won't wrinkle or smudge. The drawings show how this kind of board can be made.

Plywood is the best material for playing boards. If you know someone who does any woodworking he will probably have some odd, leftover pieces of plywood that you can use.

On boards that require lines carefully measure and mark the positions of all lines.

If you want, the board can be left unpainted, but the more pains you take with sanding and varnishing or painting, the better the finished board will look.

Go over the lines with a sharp knife, cutting a thin gouge or scratch into the wood. Then rub thinned paint over the surface. The paint will go into the lines. Let the paint dry, then sandpaper all over. The paint will come off except where it went into the lines.

Lines can also be drawn with a pencil or marking pen.

Sandpaper the wood thoroughly—especially the edges.

There are many cases where exact sizes are not given. This is because sizes will often be determined—at least to some extent—by the materials you have to work with and also by your own ideas and preferences. You may decide you want to make a larger or smaller game or puzzle than one shown on these pages.

Playing pieces can be made from all sorts of miscellaneous materials. Cut slices from a broomstick handle to get checkerlike pieces.

Golf tees fit into holes in games where pegs are used.

Wooden sticks or dowels can be cut up to get pegs of various sizes.

Buttons and coins or beans can often be used.

You may be able to find pebbles of different colors alongside streams and rivers or at the beach.

On boards that require shallow holes a drill should be used. Use a large bit and don't drill too deep.

A marble pressed into moist clay will make a neat indentation.

Rather unusual and nice-looking playing boards can be made from clay. Roll out a flat clay slab. A rolling pin or bottle will produce an even, smooth surface. Then trim the edges and make the lines or holes needed. Let the clay dry and shellac it, or if possible have it fired.

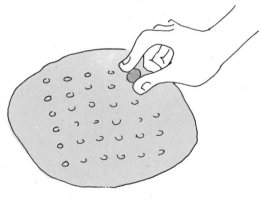

9

Fox and Geese

Two players are matched here. One is the fox, the other is seventeen geese! The fox, being a hungry and nasty fellow, wants to eat up all the geese. But as you'll see, the geese have a defense of their own.

The board is made as shown below. The fox and the geese are placed on the intersections—not inside the boxes. The fox can move in any direction. The fox "kills" a goose by jumping over him and landing on an empty intersection; the goose that has been killed is removed from the board. The fox can kill two or more geese in a series of jumps (as in checkers). And he doesn't have to make a move every time he has a turn.

The geese are not permitted to jump over the fox, and they can move only forward or to the side—not backward or on a diagonal. They win the game if they can crowd the fox into a corner so that he can't move. If the fox kills twelve of the geese he wins.

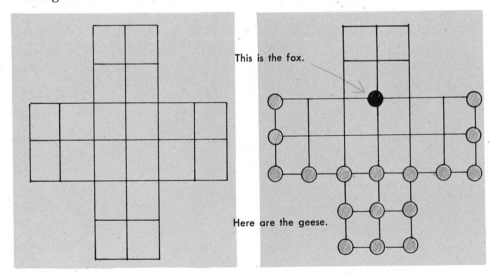

This is the fox.

Here are the geese.

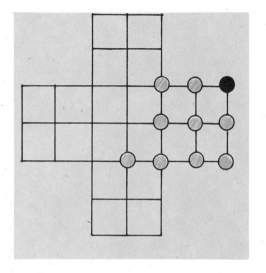

Here is a game that has been completed. Quite a few geese have been eaten by the fox, but the geese have won because the fox has been cornered.

This is a very old game played in many different forms. Sometimes it is called coyote and chickens.

You might want to experiment with your own variations. For example, you might want to try a board with a different arrangement of lines. Or you might have two foxes and more geese. How about airplanes and tanks or flies and spiders?

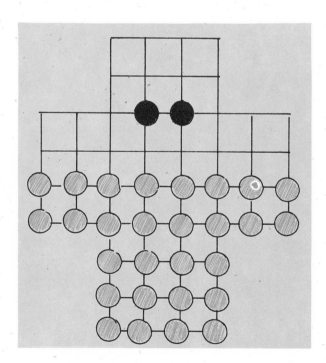

Nine-Men's Morris

This game with a strange name is one of the very oldest. If you like the idea of playing a game that dates back to at least 1400 B.C., this is the one for you. It is not unlike dara (page 5), but it is played on a different kind of board.

Each player has nine pieces and takes turns placing them on the board, one at a time. When a player has a row of three, he can remove one of his opponent's pieces. However, he cannot take a piece from an already formed row of three unless there are no other pieces to take. When all nine pieces have been placed, the game continues by moving to adjoining spots in an effort to make a line of three. A player wins if he can capture all but two of his opponent's pieces, or else block the pieces so that his opponent can't move anywhere.

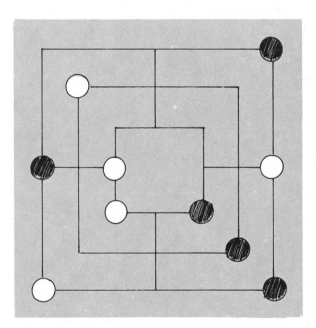

On the board are three squares, one inside another, with connecting lines. The pieces are placed at corners or where lines intersect.

You are permitted to move one of your pieces out of a line of three you have already formed. Then, on the next move, you can return the piece to its former position, making a "new" line of three—and you can remove an opponent's piece.

Here is a game in progress. Black has formed a row of three and can now remove one of white's pieces.

Words

Here's a game to give your vocabulary a workout. It is a little like Scrabble, and it can be played with as many people as you want—the more the better.

Each player has a chart of twenty-five squares. The first player calls out a letter of the alphabet—any letter. Each player writes in the letter anywhere he wants on his chart. Then the next player calls out a letter, and everyone puts it down somewhere. The object is to build as many words as possible from the letters, going up and down or across but not on the diagonal. The game continues, each player calling out a letter, until all the squares are filled. The player using the most letters to form words is the winner.

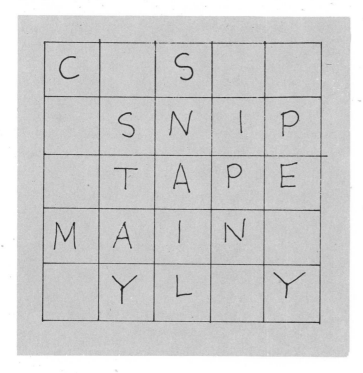

You can change the game by making more or fewer squares, or by permitting words on the diagonal as well as up and down.

This player already has five words. Can you see them?

Battleship

This is a popular and exciting game for two players. It involves the placing of four "ships" on a ruled chart. Your opponent tries to sink them by "bombing" them. This may seem like a rather complicated game, but it isn't. Once you've drawn the charts, positioned your fleet, and started to play, you'll see how simple it is and how much fun it can be.

Each player needs two charts, as shown here. On one chart you place, anywhere you choose, a four-space battleship; a three-space cruiser; and two two-space destroyers. You place the ships by making little drawings in the appropriate squares. Once they are in position you cannot move them. The other chart is used to record the bombs that you drop on the enemy navy. On this second chart you keep track of your attack—of where you've dropped your bombs.

A bomb is dropped by calling out the number and letter of a square. For example, "3-B!" drops a bomb on your opponent's 3-B square. When you drop a bomb, make a mark on your second (or enemy) chart. Each player drops four bombs with each turn. Write "1" in four places to show where you dropped your first four bombs. Use "2" as the mark for your second bombardment; and so on. Each time after the four bombs have been dropped your opponent must tell you if any of his ships have been hit, and if so, how many hits scored and on what ships. (He doesn't have to say which of the four bombs hit.)

You, as the attacker, must keep careful track of all hits

you make, in order to work out logical future attacks. If, for instance, after your second bombardment your opponent says you hit one destroyer, you should mark a "D" next to all the "2"s. Then you'll know one of those bombs hit a destroyer.

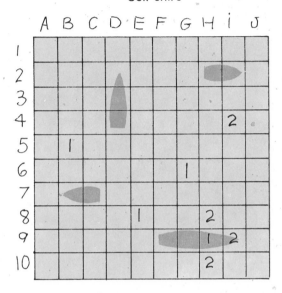

OUR SHIPS

THE ENEMY

The two charts shown on this page will give you some idea of how a game might look after a few minutes of play. Two bombardments have been made. One of the enemy's destroyers has been hit on the second bombardment. And one of our battleships has been hit twice.

It is important that neither player see the other player's chart. Some sort of barrier, such as a pile of books, must be erected between players.

A ship is sunk when it has been hit in all of its spaces. If you can sink all your opponent's ships, you win.

Squares

The object of this game is to connect dots to form squares. The game isn't as simple as it might first appear, because as the board fills up with lines many complicated possibilities develop.

The players take turns drawing lines between the dots. Two or three can play. No diagonal lines are permitted. When a player completes a square, he writes his initial in it so he knows it's his. A player who completes a square gets the chance to make another line. In this way he can sometimes complete several squares one after another.

The game can also be played with safety matches or toothpicks. Instead of drawing a line you put a stick between the dots. (The dots will have to be farther apart so that the sticks will fit between them properly.) Then, instead of putting his initial in the square, each player can have a different-colored group of beans or pebbles and put them in the squares to indicate ownership.

Can you see how the player who goes next can get a series of six boxes?

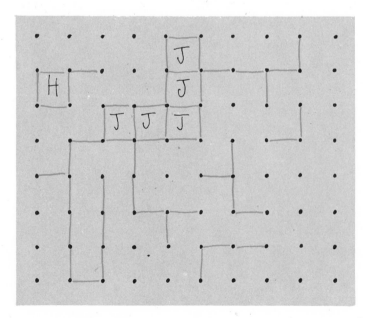

16

Skyscraper

The object of this game is to build as tall and elaborate a structure as possible using as many pieces as you can. The pieces are simply small blocks of wood. They can best be cut from a square strip. Lumber yards sell one-inch-square molding in long strips, which is ideal for this purpose. Cut the blocks carefully with a sharp saw so that the ends are straight and even. Put a sheet of sandpaper on a flat surface and rub the blocks on it so that the wood is smooth and pleasant to handle.

Keep score by counting the pieces as they are put in place. The player using the most pieces—until the skyscraper tumbles—is the winner.

Another way to play this game is with two or more people taking turns adding a piece at a time. The one who adds the last piece—the one that causes the structure to collapse—is the loser.

Make up your own rules. You can decide, for example, that every tower must include two spoons, a knife and fork, and one shoe!

You can vary the rules to permit a one-, two-, or three-block base on which to build.

Be sure to use a table that won't jiggle, or use the floor.

Watch out for curious kittens and dogs with large, wavy tails.

Ping-Pong Paddle Tennis

Even if you don't have a Ping-Pong table or a paddle tennis court, you can play a similar game—without a net —using a small, square piece of wood as your "court." The game can be played with the usual Ping-Pong ball and paddle, or you can make your own paddle and use a small rubber ball.

The player who serves has to stand behind the two-foot line. The ball is hit so that it bounces off the table, and then the other player bounces it back. A player loses the point if he misses the ball or if he doesn't hit it back onto the table. Each player takes a turn serving five times in a row. The first to get twenty-one points wins.

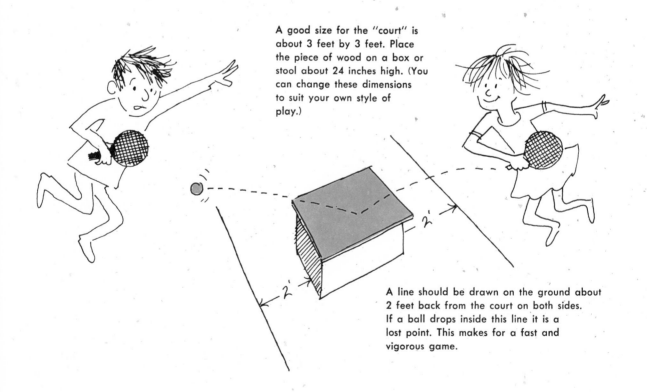

A good size for the "court" is about 3 feet by 3 feet. Place the piece of wood on a box or stool about 24 inches high. (You can change these dimensions to suit your own style of play.)

A line should be drawn on the ground about 2 feet back from the court on both sides. If a ball drops inside this line it is a lost point. This makes for a fast and vigorous game.

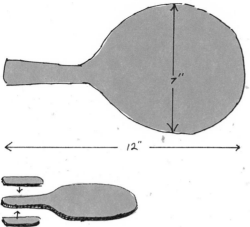

Half-inch-thick plywood is a good material for the paddles. Cut out the shape shown with a scroll saw or jigsaw. Sand it carefully.

You can glue on two separate pieces of wood to make a handle or else you can hold the handle in place with tape.

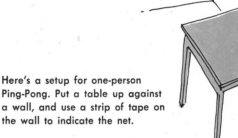

Here's a setup for one-person Ping-Pong. Put a table up against a wall, and use a strip of tape on the wall to indicate the net.

This is a kind of makeshift paddle tennis with a "net" made from cardboard cartons placed in a row. Use a small rubber ball and paddles somewhat larger than the one shown above.

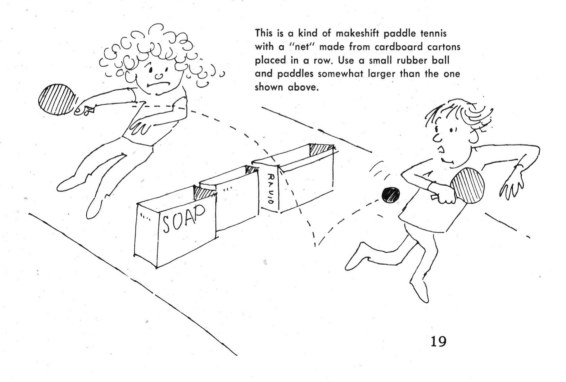

19

Sidewalk Tennis

The only equipment needed for this game is a rubber ball, a sidewalk, and . . . two players. The playing court is formed by the cracks that were put into the sidewalk when it was built. These cracks are for the purpose of controlling expansion in the summer heat. The reasoning is that since the sidewalk is going to crack, no matter how carefully built, it may as well crack along straight, neat lines. Sometimes a ribbon of asphalt is put in the cracks to offset the expansion. These cracks divide the sidewalk into boxes, and any two boxes make a playing court.

Each player has a box. The ball must be struck into your opponent's box.

If there happen to be no such sidewalks where you live, you can make your own playing court. Find any flat paved area, such as a cement or asphalt driveway or courtyard, and with a piece of chalk rule the boxes yourself.

One player bounces the ball, then hits it with his open palm into his opponent's box. The other player then hits it back into the first player's box, and the game progresses until someone misses. You can play so that each player serves five times in a row. When one player misses, the other wins a point. Another way to play is with a point going to a player only if he has been serving. When the player who has been serving misses a shot no one gets a point, but the other player gets the right to serve. Now he will get a point if his opponent misses a shot. The first player to get twenty-one points wins.

Here is another kind of sidewalk handball. It is played up against a wall. Each player has a box and any number of people can play. If the ball bounces in your box you must hit it up against the wall so that it will bounce off and into someone else's box. If you miss the ball when it is hit into your box you get a point. As soon as you get 11 points you are eliminated from the game.

Swingball Bowling

This is a kind of bowling that can be played in a small space. The bowling ball is a tennis ball attached to a string, which is then tacked to the top of an open doorway. The pins can be wooden blocks, bottles, empty tin cans, or anything that can be easily knocked over.

The ball is released and allowed to swing around past the pins. It is aimed so as to hit them on the *return* swing. The pins are arranged so that the kingpin is facing away from the bowler. You score the game by counting the number of pins knocked down. Each player can have two tries. After a player has his tries, the pins are set up again and the next player has a turn. You can also play using regular bowling rules.

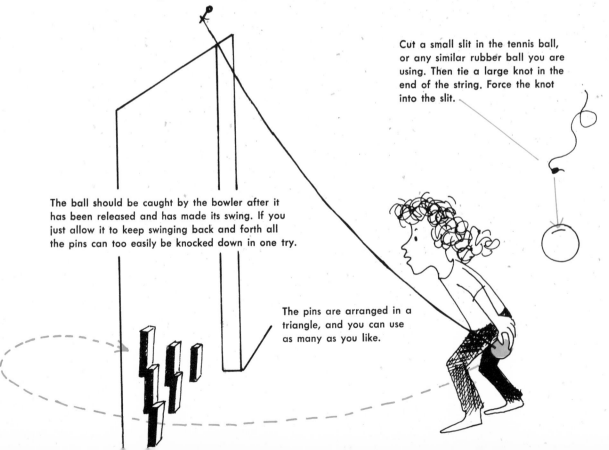

Cut a small slit in the tennis ball, or any similar rubber ball you are using. Then tie a large knot in the end of the string. Force the knot into the slit.

The ball should be caught by the bowler after it has been released and has made its swing. If you just allow it to keep swinging back and forth all the pins can too easily be knocked down in one try.

The pins are arranged in a triangle, and you can use as many as you like.

Rag Basketball

If you make a wire "basket" like the one shown here and hang it from the top of a door, you can play a simple, small-scale basketball game. It can be played by one person alone or with another player. The ball can be a bundled-up rag, or a pair of socks rolled into a ball. This kind of rag ball is better than a rubber ball if you are playing in a small room. You would have to keep chasing a rubber ball all over the place.

The wire from a wire coat hanger can be bent into this shape. A pair of pliers will help you bend it more easily.

This part fits over the top of the door.

You can hang a bucket on top of a door if you make a wire hook. (Perhaps this should be called "bucketball"?)

There are other kinds of "basketball" you can play in a small space. Hang a bucket on your doorknob and use that as a basket. If you use a rubber ball, try getting it into the basket with one bounce.

23

Miniature Golf

Half the fun of miniature golf is designing your own golf course. It can be either indoors or outdoors. If it is indoors, though, you'll find the going hard unless you have some carpeting on the floor. The ball will roll too far and too fast if you play on wood or tile. Your golf course will be more fun if there is more than one "hole." And the more varied and ingenious the obstacles you place between start and finish, the more interesting the game will be. The drawings below show some of the obstacles or traps you can use in your course. Some are for outdoor use, others for indoors.

Any number of people up to four can play. You take turns, keeping a count of the number of times you hit the ball. The player who gets from start to finish with the fewest strokes is the winner.

Each player has his own ball.

If you can't get a golf ball see if you can find a small rubber ball.

A piece of pipe or a tin can open at both ends makes a tunnel.

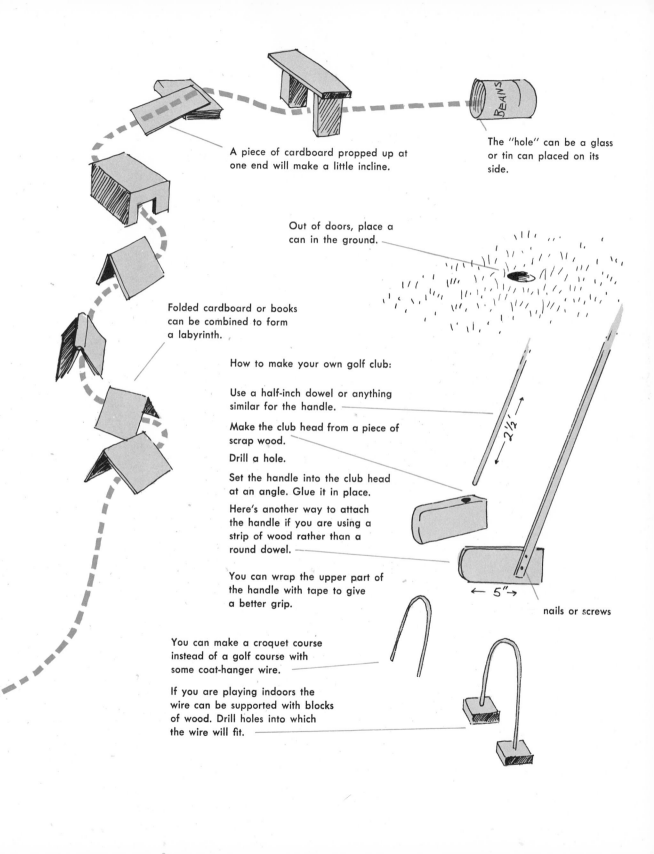

A piece of cardboard propped up at one end will make a little incline.

The "hole" can be a glass or tin can placed on its side.

BEANS

Out of doors, place a can in the ground.

Folded cardboard or books can be combined to form a labyrinth.

How to make your own golf club:

Use a half-inch dowel or anything similar for the handle.

Make the club head from a piece of scrap wood.

Drill a hole.

Set the handle into the club head at an angle. Glue it in place.

Here's another way to attach the handle if you are using a strip of wood rather than a round dowel.

You can wrap the upper part of the handle with tape to give a better grip.

2½"

5"

nails or screws

You can make a croquet course instead of a golf course with some coat-hanger wire.

If you are playing indoors the wire can be supported with blocks of wood. Drill holes into which the wire will fit.

Travel Games

The games described here are based on the movement of a piece, or man, along a path or a course to arrive at a certain destination. Each player tries to win by moving his piece to the final space first. The number of spaces to be moved at one time is determined by throwing dice or spinning a little top of some sort.

There are many commercially produced games based on this principle. But it is easy and great fun to make up your own. All you need is a large piece of paper or cardboard for the field, a few pebbles or checkers or coins, and some way of determining the number of spaces a player may move.

A spinner like this will work well. Cut the arrow out of cardboard. Hold it in place on the numbered circle with a straight pin or thumbtack. The hole in the arrow should be opened up a bit so that the arrow will spin freely when you flick it with your finger.

You can make a pair of dice from two small squares of wood.

A top with six or eight sides can be whittled from a piece of scrap wood.

A felt-tip marking pen is good for laying out the field. Use some color to liven things up a bit.

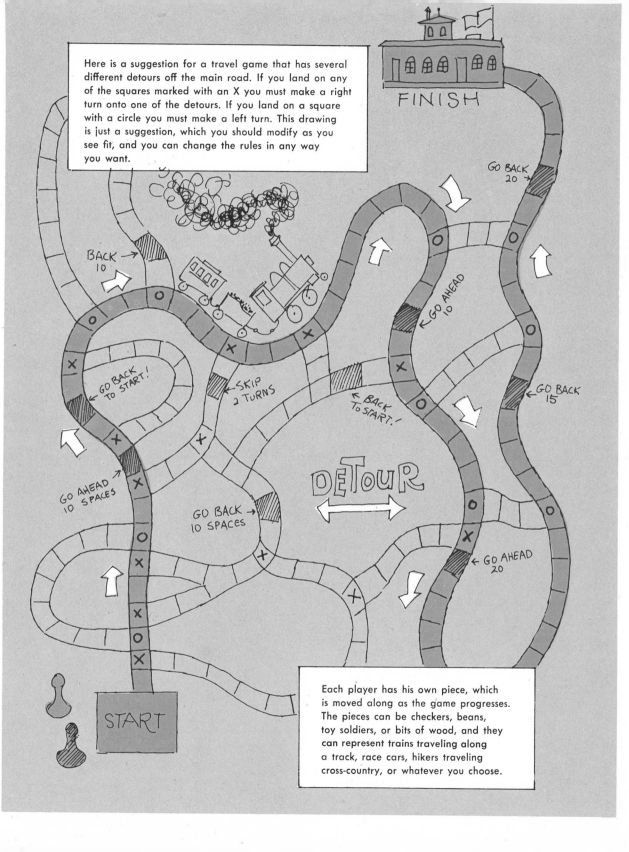

Here is a suggestion for a travel game that has several different detours off the main road. If you land on any of the squares marked with an X you must make a right turn onto one of the detours. If you land on a square with a circle you must make a left turn. This drawing is just a suggestion, which you should modify as you see fit, and you can change the rules in any way you want.

FINISH

GO BACK 20 →

BACK 10 →

← GO AHEAD 10

GO BACK 15 →

← GO BACK TO START!

↓ SKIP 2 TURNS

← BACK TO START!

DETOUR

GO AHEAD 10 SPACES →

GO BACK → 10 SPACES

← GO AHEAD 20

START

Each player has his own piece, which is moved along as the game progresses. The pieces can be checkers, beans, toy soldiers, or bits of wood, and they can represent trains traveling along a track, race cars, hikers traveling cross-country, or whatever you choose.

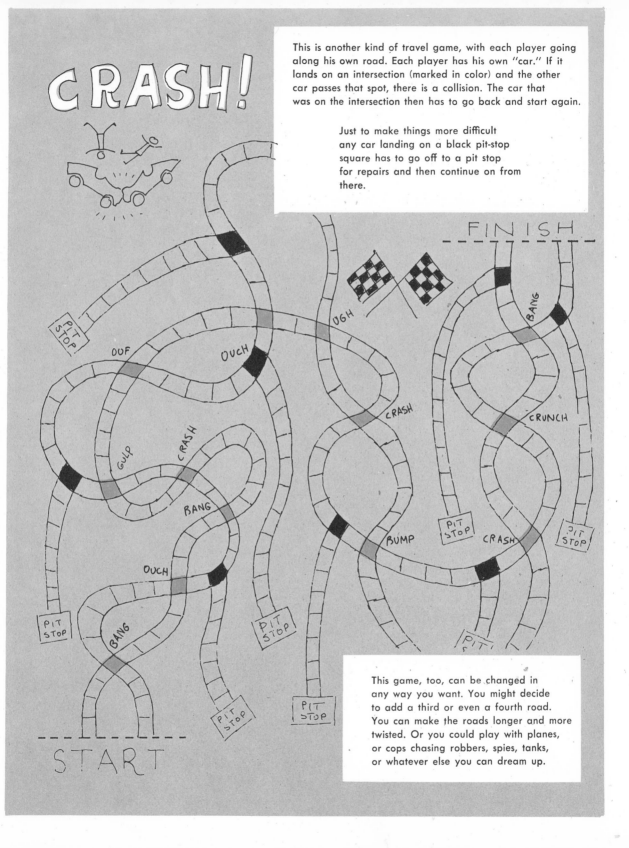

CRASH!

This is another kind of travel game, with each player going along his own road. Each player has his own "car." If it lands on an intersection (marked in color) and the other car passes that spot, there is a collision. The car that was on the intersection then has to go back and start again.

Just to make things more difficult any car landing on a black pit-stop square has to go off to a pit stop for repairs and then continue on from there.

FINISH

PIT STOP

OUF

OUCH

UGH

BANG

CRUNCH

GULP

CRASH

CRASH

BANG

BUMP

PIT STOP

CRASH

OUCH

PIT STOP

PIT STOP

PIT STOP

PIT STOP

PIT STOP

BANG

PIT STOP

PIT STOP

This game, too, can be changed in any way you want. You might decide to add a third or even a fourth road. You can make the roads longer and more twisted. Or you could play with planes, or cops chasing robbers, spies, tanks, or whatever else you can dream up.

START

Pop-It-In Games

In the games shown here, a small object is made to shoot up in the air and then land in some sort of target. The organization and layout of the game you make will be decided to some extent by the kind of materials you have to work with.

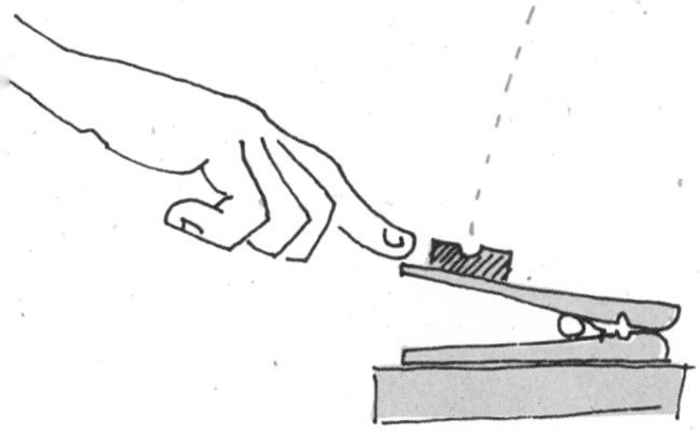

A spring clothespin will make a fine "cannon" if it is glued onto a small wood base.

Make a holder for the cannonball from a scrap of wood with a groove filed in it.

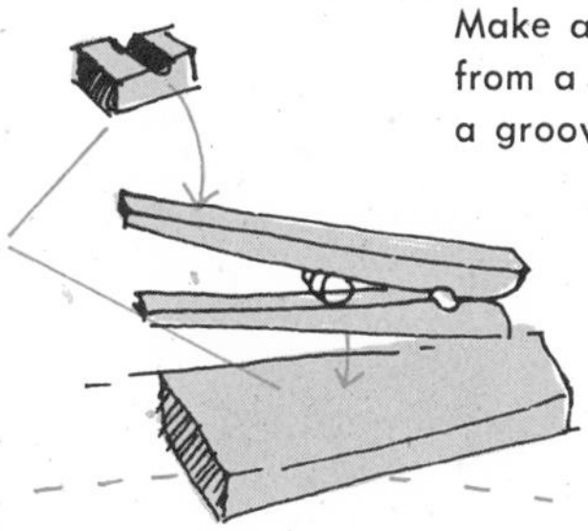

Glue in place.

Beans or small pebbles make fine cannonballs.

Set up some jars or tin cans and keep score.

With a little practice you can become quite accurate at flipping pennies with your big thumb.

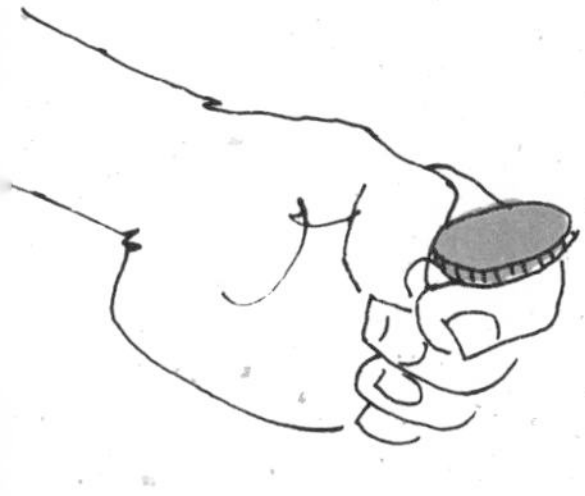

If you have a deck of cards you can play the well-known old flip-the-card-in-the-hat game. (This is the way Mississippi riverboat gamblers amused themselves when there was nobody to play with.)

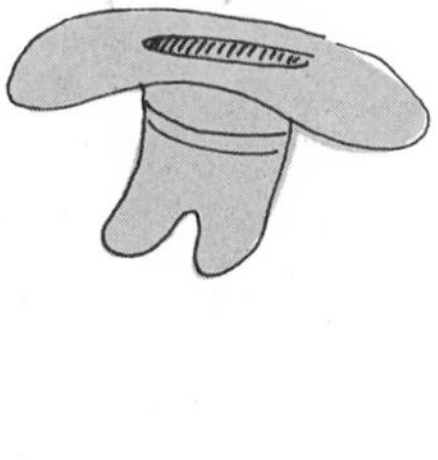

Slide Games

There are quite a few games that involve sliding a disk of some sort toward a target. Shuffleboard is one of the most popular games of this kind. You can make a simplified shuffleboard game by simply drawing a line on the ground, then trying to get your disks as near to it as possible, or on it. Each player should have three disks, and you take turns shooting. The score is totaled after all six disks have been shot. If your opponent's disk is on or near the line, one of your objectives will be to knock it away.

If you play indoors use a strip of masking tape or adhesive tape stuck to the floor. You need a smooth tile or wood or linoleum-covered floor for the disks to slide well.

You can score 5 points for the disk closest to the line and 10 points for any disk actually touching the line, or use any other scoring arrangement you see fit.

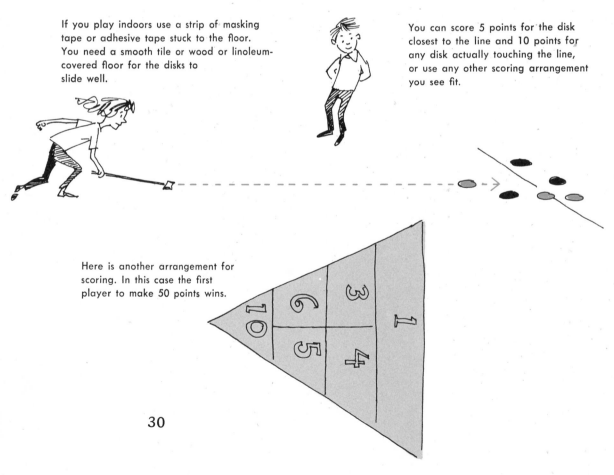

Here is another arrangement for scoring. In this case the first player to make 50 points wins.

30

The disk can be cut out of any scrap piece of board. A convenient size is about 5 inches in diameter.

The stick used to propel the disk, called a cue, can be made from any long, thin piece of wood. The curved end piece is nailed or screwed in place.

You can make up various slide games, using coins or checkers or poker chips. With small disks like these you can play on a tabletop or wood board, flipping the pieces forward with your fingertips or the palm of your hand.

There is a similar game that uses playing cards. The cards are tossed rather than slid in an effort to get them as close to the wall as possible. If they lean against the wall you get a bonus score.

Spinball

Luck, rather than skill, is the main element in this game. Four Ping-Pong balls are placed on a fenced-in board, and then an eight-sided top is set spinning on the board. The balls will fly about in the most frantic fashion as the top hits them. The balls that are knocked through the little doors are scored. If the balls are given different values, the scoring gets to be more interesting. The top can be set spinning with just a twist of the fingers. But if you make the kind of holder shown, you can get the top to turn with enormous speed and power. As a matter of fact a top and holder like this are great fun just by themselves. If the top is heavy and well balanced, it will spin for a surprisingly long time.

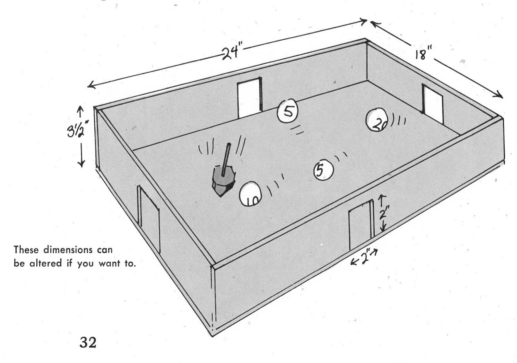

These dimensions can be altered if you want to.

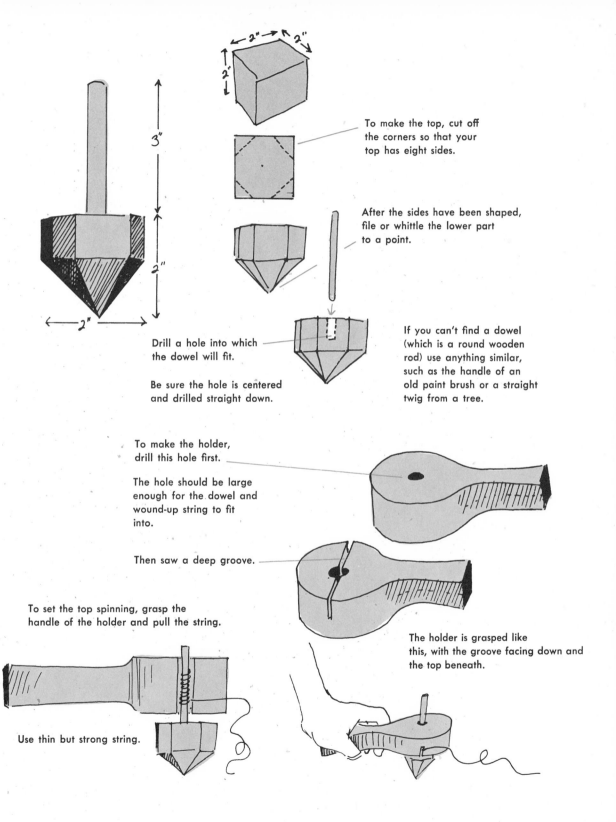

To make the top, cut off
the corners so that your
top has eight sides.

After the sides have been shaped,
file or whittle the lower part
to a point.

If you can't find a dowel
(which is a round wooden
rod) use anything similar,
such as the handle of an
old paint brush or a straight
twig from a tree.

Drill a hole into which
the dowel will fit.

Be sure the hole is centered
and drilled straight down.

To make the holder,
drill this hole first.

The hole should be large
enough for the dowel and
wound-up string to fit
into.

Then saw a deep groove.

The holder is grasped like
this, with the groove facing down and
the top beneath.

To set the top spinning, grasp the
handle of the holder and pull the string.

Use thin but strong string.

Ring Toss

This is a very easy-to-make game. It requires only a board, screw hooks, and a few rings of some sort. The object is to toss the rings onto the hooks—preferably the hooks with the higher numbers. The rings can be made from cardboard, wire, stiff rope, or any material that can be formed into a loop. The rubber rings that are used on preserve jars are perfect, if you can get some.

This kind of hook is best, but if you can't find any, a plain nail can be used.

The game of quoits is also played with rings. The rings are usually made of rope and tossed onto a peg set in the ground.

A ringer counts for 3 points. A ring that leans against the peg counts for 2. Otherwise, of all those pitched the ring that comes closest to the peg gets 1 point. A score of 21 wins.

The peg can be set into a scrap of wood for indoor play.

Splat!

You can set up your own shooting gallery for this game. The "gun" is a rubber band; the missile a folded-up piece of paper. If you hold the rubber band between your fingers as shown in the drawing, you can snap the missile forward a considerable distance and with a good deal of accuracy.

The targets are fun to make. You can cut pictures out of a magazine and paste them on pieces of cardboard. Or you can dream up your own designs.

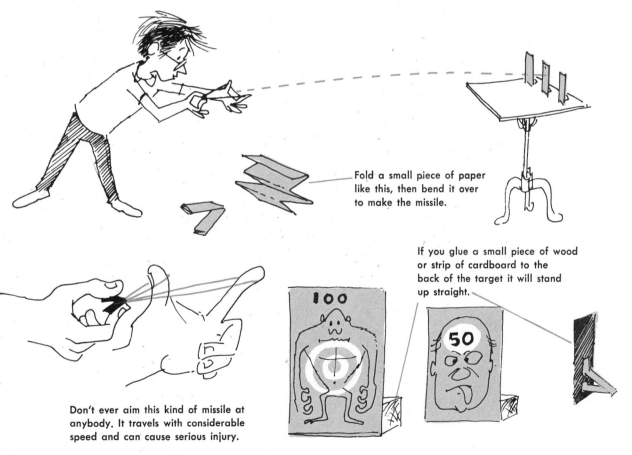

Fold a small piece of paper like this, then bend it over to make the missile.

If you glue a small piece of wood or strip of cardboard to the back of the target it will stand up straight.

100

50

Don't ever aim this kind of missile at anybody. It travels with considerable speed and can cause serious injury.

Soccer

This is the one game in the book that is fairly complicated to make. It requires some care and planning and the right materials. But you'll find the effort worthwhile because it is a fast and furious game with a lot of action. The object is to maneuver the soccer players so that they can kick the ball into the opponent's goal. It is a game for two people. To make the game, you'll need six ⅜-inch dowels (these come in 3-foot lengths); 8 feet of 1 × 4-inch board; a piece of ½-inch-thick plywood, 16 × 30 inches;

One player stands on one side and controls 1, 3, and 5. The other player, on the other side, handles 2, 4, and 6.

The dowels to which the clothespins are attached can be rotated, and also shifted back and forth.

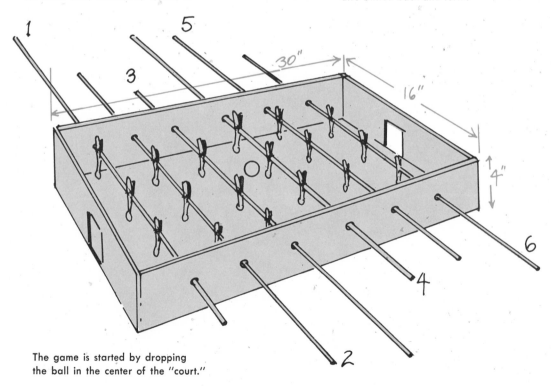

The game is started by dropping the ball in the center of the "court."

and eighteen clothespins. The old-fashioned wooden clip-type clothespins are best, though you can use the spring type if that's all you can get. You'll also need a large wooden bead or a marble to use as the soccer ball.

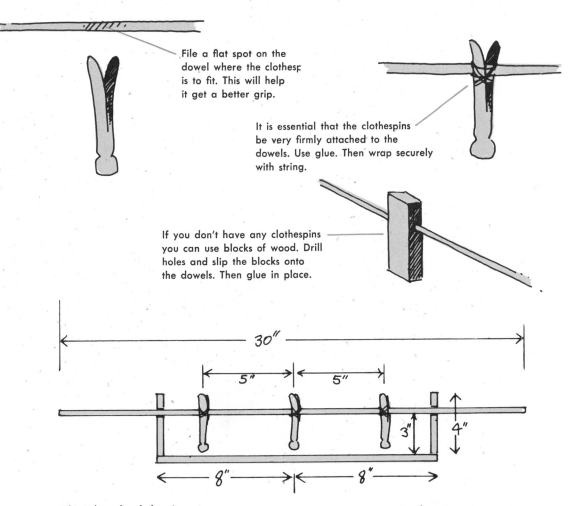

File a flat spot on the dowel where the clothesp is to fit. This will help it get a better grip.

It is essential that the clothespins be very firmly attached to the dowels. Use glue. Then wrap securely with string.

If you don't have any clothespins you can use blocks of wood. Drill holes and slip the blocks onto the dowels. Then glue in place.

This is how the clothespins should be positioned on the dowels.

Skiball

In this game a ball performs just like a ski jumper. The ball rolls down a steep incline, gathering speed, then shoots up into the air when it hits the curved section at the bottom. The target can be a box with compartments, or a series of cans, bowls, or whatever you can find that will hold the ball.

The target containers should be given numerical values so that you can keep score. Each player can take three or four shots, and then the score is totaled. The person with the highest score wins.

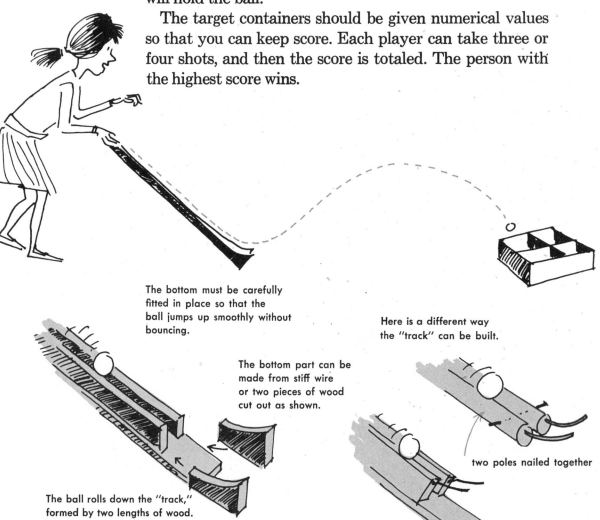

The bottom must be carefully fitted in place so that the ball jumps up smoothly without bouncing.

Here is a different way the "track" can be built.

The bottom part can be made from stiff wire or two pieces of wood cut out as shown.

two poles nailed together

The ball rolls down the "track," formed by two lengths of wood.

Marble Roll

A lot of skill and coordination are needed to get the marble from one end of this board to the other. It is very easy for the marble to fall into one of the many holes along the way.

The game can be made more or less difficult by varying the placement of the holes and the fences.

The holes should be almost as wide as the marble. A ⅜-inch hole should do it.

Thin wood strips about ¼ inch wide and about ½ inch high can be used for the edging as well as for the inside fences.

The fences could also be made from stiff cardboard.

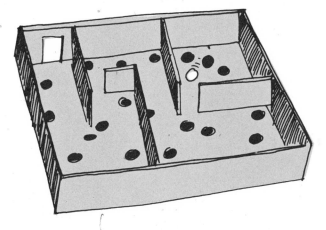

You move the marble by tipping the board back and forth.

The shape of the board doesn't have to be rectangular. A round board will also work well.

If you have a small steel ball bearing, the game can be built on a small scale.

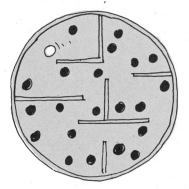

39

Pinball

A pinball machine is not difficult to make and is great fun to use. You can make one from some scrap wood, nails, a steel ball bearing or a marble, and some "bouncy" materials. Where the ball goes and how it moves about will

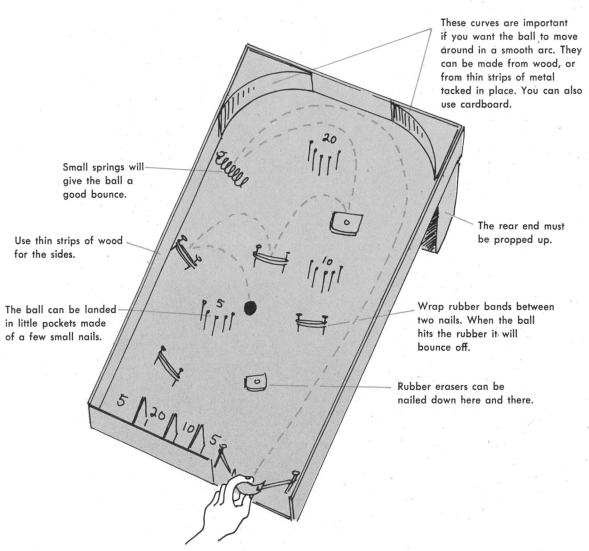

These curves are important if you want the ball to move around in a smooth arc. They can be made from wood, or from thin strips of metal tacked in place. You can also use cardboard.

Small springs will give the ball a good bounce.

Use thin strips of wood for the sides.

The ball can be landed in little pockets made of a few small nails.

The rear end must be propped up.

Wrap rubber bands between two nails. When the ball hits the rubber it will bounce off.

Rubber erasers can be nailed down here and there.

be determined by the way you place the various bouncy objects—springs, rubber erasers, or rubber bands. A few small springs tacked to the sides of the machine will cause the ball to shoot about in a very lively manner. Rubber bands stretched between nails, or hard rubber erasers, will do the same thing. There is no recommended way to arrange this kind of pinball machine. You will have to experiment with the materials you have until you get a lively, unpredictable action that causes the ball to hop all over the board, slowly working its way down to the bottom. If the ball bounces just once and then rolls right down to the bottom, you will have to figure out some changes.

An important part of this game is the method for shooting the ball up the board and getting it on its way. Some of the possibilities are shown here.

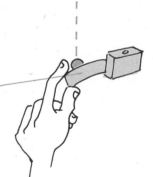

A piece of springy metal, as part of a hacksaw blade, can be nailed to a block of wood. Pull back the metal and then release it.

A small "slingshot" arrangement will work well.

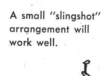

nails

rubber bands

A small piece of leather in the slingshot will hold the ball in place until you release it.

You can flip the ball with your fingers.

Memory Game

If you want to learn what kind of memory you have, try playing this game. You'll quickly find out. The game requires approximately twenty *pairs* of pictures. Any kind of pictures will do, but they must be paired. For example, two pictures of apples, or two pictures of eyes, two of automobile tires, and so on. You can cut them out of a magazine or newspaper. Then they should be pasted onto pieces of stiff, opaque paper, all cut to exactly the same size.

Two, three, or four can play. The cards are mixed up and placed face down on a table. The players take turns picking up two cards at a time. Everybody can see them. If you are lucky and happen to pick up a matching pair, you keep them. If you don't pick up a pair, you put the cards back anywhere on the table, face down. *Try to remember* where they are placed. Then the next player takes his turn. As the game progresses you will get to see most of the pictures and you will have to try and remember where the pairs are. You'll find that this is a lot more difficult than it seems. The winner is the player who collects the most pairs.

You can cut one object into two parts. This will make two pictures that can be considered a pair.

The game can also be played with a regular deck of playing cards.

Use a large table so that the cards can be well spread out.

43

Similarity

The purpose of this game is not to beat an opponent or to win. Rather, it is an exploring, conversational (or argumentative) sort of game that will give you all kinds of fresh ideas about the way different things relate to one another.

To make this game you will have to cut out a great many pictures from old magazines. The cut-outs should all be about the size of playing cards. The pictures can be of nature subjects; machines; different colors, shapes, or textures; people; furniture—anything at all. But try to get a variety. Details can be used. For example, if there is a full-page photograph of some people standing next to a car in front of a house, you might cut out the front of the car, a window of the house, and perhaps one of the people.

Spread the pictures out on a table, face up. Start by picking a picture at random. The object is to take turns placing one picture next to another that has some kind of *similarity* to it. And the fun of this game is in finding odd or unexpected similarities. For example, you might start with a picture of an automobile tire. Next to it you might have a man with glasses. (The glasses have a round shape like the tire—that is, a similarity.) Or you might use a picture of a baby carriage. (Like an automobile, it has wheels.) Or you could have a picture of a road. (That is what wheels roll on.)

As another example, suppose you had a picture of a blue airplane. Next to it you might put an open field. (The plane could land there.) Or a blue flower. (The same color.) Or an electric fan. (It also has a propeller.) Or a motorcycle. (Another means of transportation.) Or a bed. (Now, the other players would probably challenge you on this. "What's a bed got to do with an airplane?" they would ask. And you would reply, "It's obvious. The plane crashed and the pilot is going to be in bed until he recovers!") And so on.

In order for the game to be the most fun, you have to take the time to assemble a large, really varied collection of pictures—the more the better.

Para-Shoot

The object of this game is to drop a little "man" in a parachute onto a flat target or into some kind of receptacle. The parachute can be made from any thin cloth and is fastened to the parachutist by heavy thread or thin string. The slingshot that sends him on his journey can be made from a few scraps of wood and some heavy rubber bands.

The game should be played out of doors where there is plenty of room; and, if there is any kind of wind blowing, you will have to take it into account. The wind will affect the direction the chute takes as it descends.

You may be able to find a forked tree branch with a shape like this. If not you'll have to cut it out of a piece of scrap wood. One-inch-thick pine will work well.

Make sure the grain of the wood runs from top to bottom.

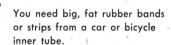

a small piece of leather with two slits

You need big, fat rubber bands or strips from a car or bicycle inner tube.

Wrap the ends very tightly with string. Be sure the rubber won't pull loose and snap you in the face.

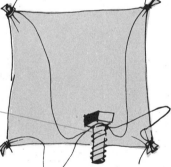

The parachutist can be a clothespin or a steel bolt, or any small, fairly heavy object.

Wrap the parachute around the parachutist to make a neat little bundle. You want the chute to go up as high as possible before it opens up. Experiment with different ways of wrapping the chute until you find an arrangement that works best.

A small cardboard carton will make a good target.

II. PUZZLES

Cut-Ups

On a piece of cardboard or heavy paper draw a cross, as shown below. Cut it up into five pieces by cutting along the dotted lines. Then see how long it takes you to form the pieces into a square. After you've done that, assemble the pieces back so that you have the original cross.

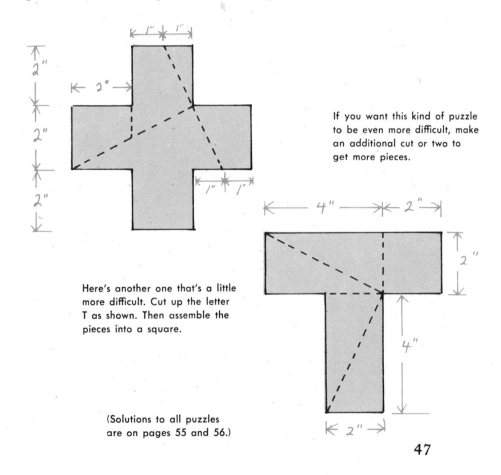

If you want this kind of puzzle to be even more difficult, make an additional cut or two to get more pieces.

Here's another one that's a little more difficult. Cut up the letter T as shown. Then assemble the pieces into a square.

(Solutions to all puzzles are on pages 55 and 56.)

Jumbled Pictures

This is a puzzle-game where you take photographs of six people and cut them up and paste them onto six blocks of wood. Each block has a part of a person on each of its six sides! The blocks are mixed up, and then you have to assemble the right pieces in the correct places to get a proper portrait. Actually this isn't a very difficult puzzle, as puzzles go, and the fun comes in combining the various parts in odd ways—one person's nose with another's chin, for example.

A block of wood about 1½ inches square is a good size, but you can go larger or smaller. You may want to make the blocks a size to suit the pictures you already have.

If you use pictures of your friends, you will probably have to get them enlarged so that they are all the same size, and so that they are large enough to fit the wood blocks.

You can make a puzzle like this using pictures cut from magazines. And the pictures don't necessarily have to be of people. You might prefer animals, or landscapes. However, the pictures should be of similar size and color and in the same general mood. Otherwise the puzzle is too easy.

Shift It

Draw eight boxes and place three pennies and three nickels as shown. Now see if you can get the three pennies in the three lefthand boxes and the three nickels in the righthand boxes. No jumping permitted. Anybody can do this eventually. The trick is to do it in the fewest possible moves!

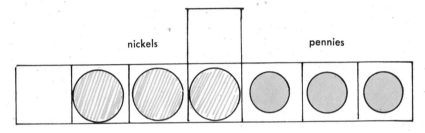

Line-Up

Get ten small objects the same size, such as pennies, beans, or checkers, and see if you can arrange them to make five rows with four objects in each row.

Another, similar puzzle requires twelve objects. See if you can make six rows with four objects in each row.

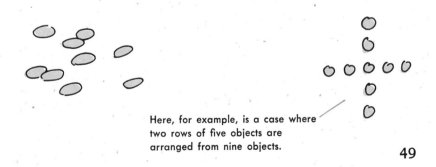

Here, for example, is a case where two rows of five objects are arranged from nine objects.

Stick Puzzles

These puzzles are played with any small sticks that are all the same size. Wooden safety matches work fine, or you can use toothpicks.

Arrange twelve sticks as shown. Now see if you can get three squares by shifting only three sticks.

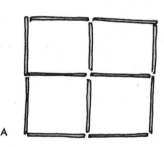

A

Arrange eight sticks so as to get two squares and four triangles.

B

Arrange seven sticks as shown here. Now form three connected triangles by moving only four of the sticks.

C

Change the arrangement shown here so as to get four boxes. But you can shift only three sticks.

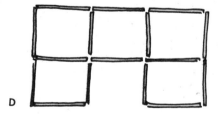

D

One Line

All you need for this puzzle is a pencil and a piece of paper. Draw the set of triangles shown here, using one continuous line. Don't take the pencil off the paper and don't go over a line once it is drawn.

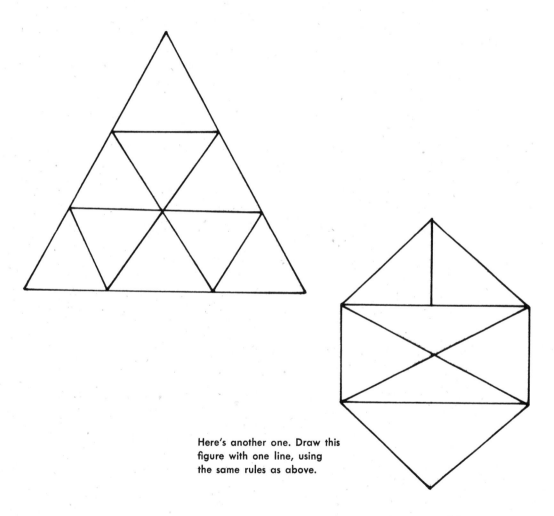

Here's another one. Draw this figure with one line, using the same rules as above.

String and Stick

The object of this puzzle is to get the string loop and the stick it is attached to fastened to the buttonhole of a shirt or jacket, as shown in the drawing. You are not permitted to untie or cut the string, of course.

Once you've figured out how this is done, you can have a great time fastening it to your friends' clothing (not letting them watch you do it), then asking them to remove it.

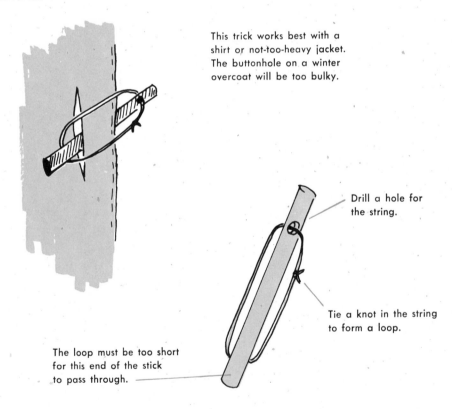

This trick works best with a shirt or not-too-heavy jacket. The buttonhole on a winter overcoat will be too bulky.

Drill a hole for the string.

Tie a knot in the string to form a loop.

The loop must be too short for this end of the stick to pass through.

Peg Puzzle

This is a tough one that will keep you busy for some time. Start with all the pegs in their holes and only the center hole empty. Then select any peg and jump it horizontally or vertically over another peg, being sure to land in an empty hole. Every time you jump over a peg it is removed. The object is to end up with all the pegs removed except one in the center hole.

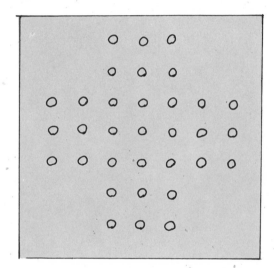

Locate the holes as shown here.

Drill the holes slightly larger than the pegs so that they can be easily inserted and taken out.

Don't drill the holes all the way through.

You can make the pegs from short lengths of ¼-inch-diameter dowels, or any similar sticks.

You can also draw this board on a piece of paper or cardboard and play with beans or pebbles instead of pegs.

53

Bull Pen

In this game there are six bulls, each of which belongs in his own pen. However, there is one extra pen, marked with an X, which makes shifting around possible. You can use checkers or blocks of wood or pieces of cardboard for the bulls. The pens can be drawn on a piece of cardboard. Position the bulls (each one of which is numbered) as shown in the drawing, and see how long it takes you to get them where they are supposed to be.

No more than one bull at a time in any of the pens.

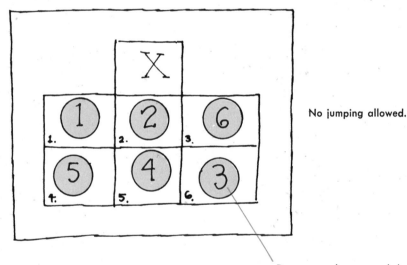

No jumping allowed.

Draw a number on each bull.

54

Solutions to Puzzles

CUT-UPS

 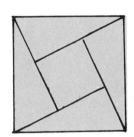

LINE-UP

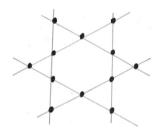 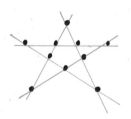

STICK PUZZLES

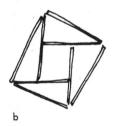  

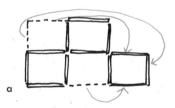

a

b

c

d

ONE LINE

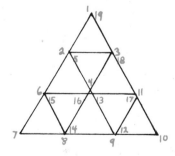 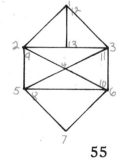

STRING AND STICK

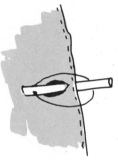

To put in place:

1. Bunch up the cloth around the buttonhole. Slip the string loop over the cloth as shown.

2. Put the stick through the buttonhole.

3. Smooth out the cloth. The stick is now in place, as shown.

To remove:

1. Bunch up the cloth around the buttonhole. Pull the loop downward.

2. Pull the stick out of the buttonhole.

PEG PUZZLE

The holes are numbered as shown in the drawing on the right. The sequence of moves listed below will leave only one peg in the center hole.

5 to 17, 12 to 10, 3 to 11, 18 to 6, 1 to 3,
3 to 11, 30 to 18, 27 to 25, 24 to 26, 13 to 27,
27 to 25, 22 to 24, 31 to 23, 16 to 28, 33 to 31,
31 to 23, 4 to 16, 7 to 9, 10 to 8, 21 to 7, 7 to 9,
24 to 10, 10 to 8, 8 to 22, 22 to 24, 24 to 26,
19 to 17, 16 to 18, 11 to 25, 26 to 24, 29 to 17.

```
        1     2     3
        •     •     •

        4     5     6
        •     •     •

7   8   9  10  11  12  13
•   •   •   •   •   •   •

14  15  16  17  18  19  20
•   •   •   •   •   •   •

21  22  23  24  25  26  27
•   •   •   •   •   •   •

       28    29    30
        •     •     •

       31    32    33
        •     •     •
```

About Harvey Weiss

Harvey Weiss has written and illustrated many books for children, among them *The Gadget Book, How to Make Your Own Books, Model Airplanes and How to Build Them, Model Cars and Trucks and How to Build Them, Motors and Engines and How They Work,* and *Ship Models and How to Build Them.* He is, as well, a distinguished sculptor whose work has received many awards and has been exhibited in galleries and museums across the country. A dedicated tinkerer and gadgeteer—his latest creation is a very handsome, very complicated, and wholly impractical steam-powered model airplane—Mr. Weiss brings to his books a sure sense of what appeals to and can be accomplished by young people, and a sculptor's eye for simple, uncluttered forms.

An assistant professor of sculpture at Adelphi University, Mr. Weiss lives in Greens Farms, Connecticut.